SHORT WALKS MAD

LAKE DIST

Contents

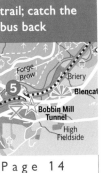

Walk 1

KESWICK
RAILWAY
PATH

Distance
4.1 miles/6.6km

Time
2½ hours   CATCH A BUS

Start/Finish
Keswick/Threlkeld

Parking CA12 5EL
Pay-and-display at start

Cafés/pubs
Keswick, Threlkeld

**Access-for-all
trail; catch the
bus back**

Forge
Brow   Briery

5   Blencat

Bobbin Mill
Tunnel

High
Fieldside

Page 14

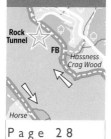

Walk 5

GRASMERE

Distance
3.8 miles/6.1km

Time
2 hours

Start/Finish
Grasmere village

Parking LA22 9SJ
Pay-and-display at start

Cafés/pubs
Grasmere village

Treat yourself to
some Grasmere
Gingerbread

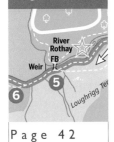

Walk 6

ESKDALE

Distance
2 miles/3.2km

Time
1 hour

Start/Finish
Dalegarth for Boot
Station

Parking CA19 1TF
Pay-and-display at start

Cafés/pubs
Café at station; pubs
in Boot

Somewhere
quieter; steam
railway ride

Walk 7

WRAY CASTLE & BLELHAM TARN

Distance
4.7 miles/7.6km

Time
2¾ hours TAKE A FERRY

Start/Finish
Wray Castle

Parking LA22 0JA
Pay-and-display at start

Cafés/pubs
National Trust café

Top NT property
and wetland
nature reserve

Walk 8	Walk 9	Walk 10

GRIZEDALE FOREST

Distance
5 miles/8.1km

Time
2¾ hours

Start/Finish
Grizedale Visitor Centre

Parking LA22 0QJ
Pay-and-display at start

Cafés/pubs
Visitor centre café

Woodland wildlife and sculpture trail

CONISTON

Distance
2.9 miles/4.6km

Time
1½ hours

Start/Finish
Coniston Boating Centre

Parking LA21 8AN
Pay-and-display at start

Cafés/pubs
At start; Coniston

Ruskin Museum and water speed records

RAVENGLASS

Distance
2.2 miles/3.5km

Time
1¼ hours   GO BY TRAIN

Start/Finish
Ravenglass

Parking CA18 1SQ
Pay-and-display at start

Cafés/pubs
Café at steam railway station; Ravenglass

Lakeland's seaside and Roman ruins

GETTING OUTSIDE
IN THE LAKE DISTRICT

River Lowther

"

Pooh sticks,
rope swings and
lichen galore!

What more do
you want from a
family explore...
Ice cream?

Well, it has this
too!

OS GetOutside Champion
Craig and his family

A very warm welcome to the new Short Walks Made Easy guide to the Lake District National Park – what a fantastic selection of leisurely walks we have for you!

The Lake District, known to locals as Lakeland, is home to many large lakes, such as Buttermere, Grasmere and Coniston. Coupled with jaw-dropping mountain backdrops, the lakes are the perfect place to have a wander and watch the world go by. Their shores also offer water-based activities and picnic spots.

Here, nature is thriving, and on any of these walks you're likely to see goldfinches, woodpeckers and dippers among much other wildlife, and, if you're lucky, otters, roe deer and red squirrels. Don't forget your binoculars!

There's plenty of history to uncover in the National Park, especially along the Keswick Railway Path, at Wray Castle and at Ravensdale's Roman Bath House. You're never more than a short drive away from a village or town where you can pick up local delicacies, such as gingerbread, damson jam and Cumberland sausage!

One of my favourite Lake District days out involves a short walk along Ullswater's shore from Glenridding to Aira Force. Fuel up with a coffee at the National Trust café, and continue your stroll around Aira Force itself to admire the waterfall. As you make your way back to Glenridding, look out onto the lake to spot the iconic 160-year-old 'steamers', or catch one back to town if you wish. Finish your walk with a bite to eat at The Inn on the Lake, which offers a variety of menus, all in a beautiful setting.

Craig Henderson
OS GetOutside Champion

WE SMILE MORE
WHEN WE'RE OUTSIDE

Buttermere

Whether it's a short walk during our lunch break or a full day's outdoor adventure, we know that a good dose of fresh air is just the tonic we all need.

At Ordnance Survey (OS), our passion is to help more people to get outside more often. Through our GetOutside initiative, we aim to help you lead an active outdoor lifestyle, so that you can live longer, stay younger and enjoy life more.

Just as the outdoors is for everyone, GetOutside is for everyone, and we hope to bring you the very best of Great Britain. We are blessed with an island that is beautiful and unique, and our trusted source of inspirational content is bursting with ideas for places to go, things to do and easy beginner's guides on how to get started. It can be daunting when you're new to something, so we want to bring you the know-how from the people who live and breathe the outdoors.

To help guide us, our team of awe-inspiring OS GetOutside Champions share their favourite places to visit, hints and tips for outdoor adventures, as well as tried and tested accessible, family and wheelchair-friendly routes. We hope that you will feel inspired to spend more time outside and reap the physical and mental health benefits that the outdoors has to offer. With our handy guides, paper and digital mapping, and exciting new apps, we can be with you every step of the way.

To find out more visit GetOutside.uk

A WARM NATIONAL PARK WELCOME

Lake District National Park

The Lake District is England's largest national park and home to the country's highest mountain, Scafell Pike. But you don't have to scale the high fells (mountains) to enjoy your Lake District adventure.

The carefully chosen walks in this guide seek out the gentler side of the Lake District, each packed with breathtaking views – this really is a spectacular part of Britain.

Covering the National Park from Buttermere to Ullswater and Ravenglass to Grizedale, these picturesque, low-level routes are very simple to follow and provide accessible walks for all the family. There's lots of variety and much to see: the stunning scenery of the Greta Gorge along the old railway line from Keswick to an off-the-tourist trail wander in Eskdale, there really is something to suit everyone.

These routes are ideal for beginners to country walking who want an easily signposted circular walk as part of a day out in the Lake District for the whole family, or just for anyone who prefers a low-level, accessible walk.

We've made it as easy as possible to plan your Lake District visit in advance. From checking how busy popular sites are within the National Park to further exploration on our range of "Miles without Stiles" walks, everyone is welcome.

How will you enjoy the Lake District National Park?

Lake District National Park Authority
www.lakedistrict.gov.uk

RESPECTING
THE COUNTRYSIDE

You can't beat getting outside in the British countryside, but it's vital that we leave no trace when we're enjoying the great outdoors.

Let's make sure that generations to come can enjoy the countryside just as we do.

Leave no trace

Keep dogs under control; bin and bag waste

Do not light fires; only BBQ at official sites

Leave gates as you find them

Keep to footpaths and open access land

Plan ahead for your trip

For more details please visit www.gov.uk/countryside-code

USING THIS GUIDE

Easy-to-follow National Park walks for everyone

Before setting off

Check the walk information panel to plan your outing

- Consider using **Public transport** where flagged. If driving, note the satnav postcode for the car park under **Parking**
- The suggested **Time** is based on a gentle pace
- Note the availability of **Cafés**, tearooms and pubs, and **Toilets**

Terrain and hilliness

- **Terrain** indicates the nature of the route surface
- Any rises and falls are noted under **Hilliness**

Walking with your dog?

- This panel states where **Dogs** *must* be on a lead and how many stiles there are – in case you need to lift your dog

A perfectly pocket-sized walking guide

- Handily sized for ease of use on each walk
- When not being read, it fits nicely into a pocket…
- …so between points, put this book in the pocket of your coat, trousers or day sack and enjoy your stroll in glorious national park countryside – we've made it pocket-sized for a reason!

Flexibility of route presentation to suit all readers

- **Not comfortable map reading?** Then use the simple-to-follow route profile and accompanying route description and pictures
- **Happy to map read?** New-look walk mapping makes it easier for you to focus on the route and the points of interest along the way
- Read the insightful **Did you know?, Local legend, Stories Behind the Walk** and **Nature Notes** to help you make the most of your day out and to enjoy all that each walk has to offer

The easy-to-use walk map

- **Large-scale** mapping for ultra-clear route finding

- **Numbered points** key turns along the route tie in with the route instructions and respective points marked on the profile

- **Pictorial symbols** for intuitive map reading, see Map Symbols on the front cover flap

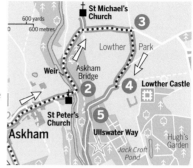

The simple-to-follow walk profile

- Progress easily along the route using the illustrative profile, it has **numbered points** for key turning points and **graduated distance** markers

- Easy-read **route directions** with turn-by-turn detail

- Reassuring **route photographs** for each numbered point

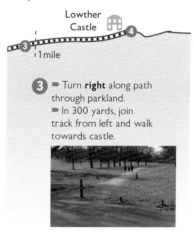

Many of the features and symbols shown are taken from Ordnance Survey's celebrated **Explorer** mapping, designed to help people across Great Britain enjoy leisure time spent outside. For more on this – and how you can start planning your own walks and adventures, please see the inside back cover.

KESWICK RAILWAY PATH

The Keswick Railway Path follows the route of the former Cockermouth, Keswick and Penrith Railway through the delightful, wooded gorge cut by the River Greta between Keswick and Threlkeld. Railway enthusiasts will find plenty of interest, including reopened tunnels and old workers' huts, while wildlife watchers should be able to spot a variety of birds and mammals in the woods and along the riverbanks. Walk as far as Threlkeld and then catch the bus back to Keswick.

Distance
4.1 miles/6.6km

Time
2½ hours

Parking
Keswick: Bell Close car park, CA12 5EL Threlkeld: Blease Road car park, CA12 4RX

Start
Keswick Bus Station (opposite entrance to Booths supermarket)

Finish
Bus stop in Threlkeld, at junction of Station Road and Main St

Public toilets
Keswick, Threlkeld

Cafés/pubs
Keswick, Threlkeld

Terrain
Surfaced old railway path

Hilliness
Mostly level, slight inclines

Footwear
All year

The Keswick Railway Path is a multi-use trail

Did you know? Postman Pat stamps were issued in March 2020, affixed to specially designed envelopes and postmarked at Keswick on the first day that the stamps were issued.

Local legend A curiosity of the Keswick line lies just beyond Threlkeld. Highgate Platform opened in 1908 for the sole purpose of allowing a small number of children to attend Mungrisdale School. Just two trains stopped each day – one at 8am and the other at 4pm. There was no platform sign as the train company did not want to encourage other passengers to leave the train. It closed in 1929. Nothing remains today.

The view from Latrigg; the path skirts the woods at the bottom of the hill

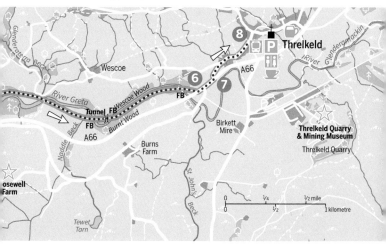

STORIES BEHIND
THE WALK

Blencathra There are several good views of Blencathra from the railway path, the best coming soon after walkers emerge from the first tunnel. A key feature of this fell, one of the Lake District's highest, is its arêtes – the narrow, rocky ridges that make it a favourite with scramblers. The most famous of these is Sharp Edge.

River Greta and Storm Desmond

The River Greta is fed by streams (known locally as becks) that flow off the surrounding fells. The river reached its highest ever recorded level in December 2015 – as a result of Storm Desmond – flooding Keswick and ripping out sections of the railway path. It took five years for the path to be repaired and cost of £7.9 million. Bridges had to be rebuilt, embankments stabilised and the path reconstructed. In addition, the Bobbin Mill tunnel, closed since the 1970s, was reinstated.

☆ Leisure
Centre

½ mile

With your back to bus station and supermarket car park, turn **left along The Headlands.
Go **left again at junction with Tithebarn Street/ Heads Road.

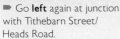

1 ** Turn **right** at mini-roundabout.
** Follow road for 500 yards – round two sharp bends.

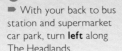

Cockermouth, Keswick and Penrith Railway

The 31-mile Cockermouth, Keswick and Penrith Railway was built by Thomas Bouch in 1865. It linked up with existing lines to provide a direct route to bring coke from the Durham coal mines to the iron-making industry on the west coast and, in turn, transport Cumberland coal back to the blast furnaces of the north-east. Industrial traffic was gradually replaced by passengers as Lake District tourism took off in the 20th century. The line was eventually closed in 1972, although some of the original infrastructure remains, including bridges and tunnels.

Threlkeld village

Threlkeld, which sits at the foot of Blencathra, has probably been settled since prehistoric times, although the modern village owes its existence to mineral extraction. Lead and zinc were mined from the 17th century until the 1920s, while granite was quarried until the 1980s.

Bobbin Mill Tunnel · Blencathra

1 mile · 1½ miles

2 ➡ Turn **left** along Station Road (war memorial on opposite corner).

3 ➡ As Brundholme Road goes right, keep **straight ahead**. ➡ Immediately turn **left** along path towards leisure centre and then pass to **right** of building.

4 ➡ At back of leisure centre, turn **right**. ➡ Beyond parking area and old station platform, join route of former railway and stroll for 1 mile.

NATURE NOTES

The Keswick Railway Path is bordered by wildlife-rich woods while the Greta also attracts a variety of species. Watch for **treecreepers** crawling up and down tree trunks and **dippers** bobbing up and down on rocks in the river. In the spring, **sand martins** nest in holes in the riverbank. **Red squirrels** can be spotted all year round. The Greta gorge is relatively damp, so the woodland floor and some tree trunks are blanketed with **mosses**. Spindly **birch trees** are among the species growing beside the path.

Birch trees are often found along river banks

Sand martins fly in from Africa, nest in colonies and are common visitors

Ferns and mosses are an indicator of clean air. Note the distinctive woodland smells

2 miles

2½ miles

5 ➡ Near A66 viaduct, route passes through lit tunnel.
➡ Continue for just over 2 miles on shared-use path, following River Greta upstream.

6 ➡ After path uses zig-zags to climb to A66, turn **left** along pavement.

Squirrel Nutkin, one of Beatrix Potter's most popular creations, has a stronghold around Derwent Water

Underwater bugs are stalked by dippers who love fast-flowing water

Watch out for treecreepers hunting for insects

3 miles   3½ miles

P Threlkeld

Public Toilets

Threlkeld Coffee Shop

Horse & Farrier

7 ➡ Take next road on **left** – towards Threlkeld village.

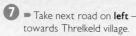

8 ➡ Bus stop for X5 back to Keswick is at junction with Station Road (on **right**) after 600 yards. This is few yards short of Threlkeld Coffee Shop (signposted to right).

Walk 1 Keswick Railway Path   **19**

LOWTHER CASTLE

Following quiet lanes and waymarked paths, this walk explores the rolling countryside of the Lowther Valley. Walkers set off from the idyllic village of Askham, cross the parkland surrounding Lowther Castle and stroll beside the banks of the sedate River Lowther. This area, as the names suggest, has long been associated with the Lowthers, a family who can trace their roots back to the 12th century.

Distance	3.7 miles/6km
Time	2¼ hours
Start/Finish	Askham
Parking CA10 2PF	Village car park in Askham
Public toilets	None
Cafés/pubs	In Askham
Terrain	Lanes and clear tracks and paths
Hilliness	One steady climb between points ➋ and ➌ continuing as a gentle rise to ➍ after which there's a descent to ➎
Footwear	All year ⬗

Did you know? During World War II, the garden at Lowther Castle was paved over with concrete in order to test and develop Matilda tanks. The Candle Defence Light was fitted to see if by blinding the enemy with flickering lights on night-time operations would significantly reduce infantry casualties. Although Eisenhower and Churchill witnessed a demonstration, the system never entered active service.

Local legend James Lowther, 1st Earl of Lonsdale, would be worthy of an episode of *Horrible Histories*. By all accounts (and there are plenty of them), he was a thoroughly unpleasant character. Perhaps his greatest claim to the sobriquet of Wicked Jimmy was, despite being married, he fell in love with the daughter of a tenant. When she died in 1761, he could not bear to have her buried and insisted that her body was kept in bed until the putrefaction became unbearable. He then had her body placed in a glass topped coffin and kept in a cupboard. She was buried seven weeks later.

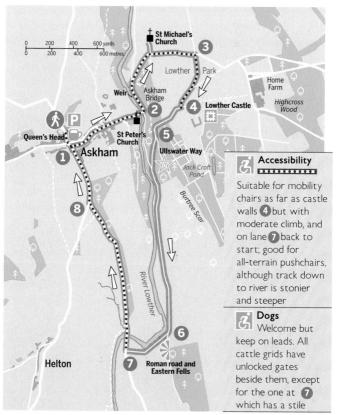

Accessibility

Suitable for mobility chairs as far as castle walls ❹ but with moderate climb, and on lane ❼ back to start; good for all-terrain pushchairs, although track down to river is stonier and steeper

Dogs

Welcome but keep on leads. All cattle grids have unlocked gates beside them, except for the one at ❼ which has a stile

STORIES BEHIND THE WALK

† St Michael's Church

Askham has two churches. St Michael's is on the left as the road climbs from the River Lowther early in the walk. The grounds contain the substantial mausoleum of William Lowther, Earl of Lonsdale, who died in 1844. There are also statues of and memorials to other members of the Lowther family inside the church.

☆ **Ullswater Way** Parts of this walk follow the Lowther Castle Loop. This is a circular add-on to the Ullswater Way, a 20-mile waymarked route round England's second largest natural lake. Serious hikers aim to walk it in a day, but you can also hop on and off the Ullswater 'Steamers' or local buses to complete it in shorter, linear chunks.

P

Queen's Head

St Peter's Church †

St Michael's Church †

1 ➡ Ignore lane on left beside pub, but immediately after Askham Stores on corner, turn **left**, signposted 'Lowther', and walk to St Peter's Church.

➡ Leave car park by vehicle entrance and turn **left** along road towards Queen's Head pub.

2 ➡ Beyond church, road crosses River Lowther and then climbs to reach St Michael's Church.
➡ In about 400 yards reach a clear path on right.

Lowther Castle

Lowther Castle was built for William Lowther in 1814, largely with money made from coal mining in west Cumberland. The family's wealth dwindled significantly in the first few decades of the 20th century, largely due to the ostentatious lifestyle of the fifth earl, and they were forced to dismantle the castle in 1957. Tourists can now visit the shell of the building and its gardens and grounds.

Roman Road

As the route reaches an open area at **6**, walkers are treated to a particularly good view of the eastern fells. Nearly 2,000 years ago, the Romans built a road that followed this long ridge line, reaching its highest point on Racecourse Hill, or High Street, at 2,716 feet (828m) above sea level. The road linked the forts of Galava, now Ambleside, and Brovacum (Brougham).

Lowther Castle

3 — **4**

1 mile

Ullswater Way ☆

5

3 ➡ Turn **right** along path through parkland.
➡ In 300 yards, join track from left and walk towards castle.

4 ➡ Turn **right** at signposted path junction in front of north gate.
➡ Cross cattle grid to enter woods and follow stony track downhill for 400 yards to path joining from right.

Walk 2 Lowther Castle **23**

NATURE NOTES

The woods, parkland and fields along this edge of the Lake District are home to a varied array of wildlife. Even if you don't see them, there's a good chance you'll hear **great spotted woodpeckers** tapping on the trees or the high-pitched, plaintive call of **buzzards**. Smaller birds include **coal tits** and **nuthatches**. The latter can often be spotted moving up and down tree trunks. Watch too for **hares** and **roe deer**, although both move very quickly once aware of humans.

Hares are making a welcome return to the Lake District. Mainly nocturnal, the best chance of spotting one is early in the morning

Technically challenging, the Lowther is one of the best fisheries for brown trout in Cumbria

Roman road and Eastern Fells

6 ☀ 7

2 miles

5 ➡ Keep **left** here. (You now follow waymarked 'Lowther Castle Loop' as far as road **7**.)
➡ Soon leave woods and walk to path fork in ¾ mile.

6 ➡ Branch **right** beside River Lowther.
➡ Follow river to lane.

With a wingspan of up to 1.5 metres, you can't fail to spot buzzards often being mobbed by crows

Nuthatches are unique in going down a tree trunk head first seeking out hidden seeds

The meadow brown butterfly is a common sight from mid-June to mid-August: they like the grasses alongside the path

3 miles

8 Queen's Head 🍺 🅿

7 ➤ Turn **right** along minor road, reaching next lane junction in ¾ mile.

8 ➤ Turn **right** again towards Askham.
➤ After passing Askham Stores, retrace steps to car park entrance, set back on right 70 yards beyond pub.

Opposite (clockwise): Herdwick tup, Eskdale; Hartsop field barn, Ullswater;
Buttermere; Storrs Hall, Windermere; Hindscarth Edge, Buttermere.
This page (clockwise): Steam Yacht Gondola, Coniston; Windermere; Throstle Garth
pack horse bridge, Eskdale; Tilberthwaite Farm cottage, Coniston.

BUTTERMERE

This lakeside walk takes place in the most spectacular of surroundings. As you pass in and out of woods and through meadows that fringe the shores of Buttermere, rocky slopes rear up steeply on either side of the water. The paths are easy to follow and mostly good underfoot. A short, unlit tunnel cut through the rock provides some excitement on the return route, but watch your head on its low roof!

Distance	4.3 miles/6.9km
Time	2½ hours
Start/Finish	Buttermere village
Parking CA13 9UZ	Lake District National Park pay-and-display car park behind Bridge Hotel, Buttermere village
Public toilets	Buttermere car park
Cafés/pubs	In Buttermere
Terrain	Lake shore path/ track
Hilliness	Mostly level to ❻; gently undulating after that with steps after ❼
Footwear	All year ⟫

Did you know? Perhaps the most famous fellwalker was Alfred Wainwright (1907-1991) who wrote and illustrated 'pictorial guides' covering the Lake District. Look out for his memorial in St James' Church.

Local legend The fact that the Lake District became such a honeypot for the poets of the romantic era rests in part to the natural charms of Mary Robinson, the "Maid of Buttermere". She grew up in the Fish Inn and was only 15 when she was 'discovered'. Wordsworth was struck by her simple and natural way of life. It did not end well for Mary though as she fell victim to a fraudster. There are many novels about her.

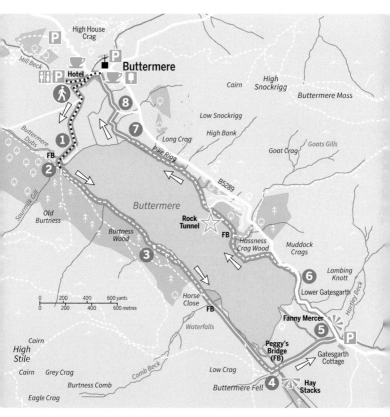

STORIES BEHIND
THE WALK

Ayrshire ice creams Syke Farm, on the edge of Buttermere village, uses its own herd of Ayrshires to make the ice cream on sale at its café. These dairy cows – white with reddy-brown patches – produce milk that is high in butterfat, making it particularly suitable for making into cheese, yoghurt and ice cream.

Fanny Mercer The white cross on the lower slopes of Fleetwith Edge, the steep ridge leading almost directly up from Gatesgarth Farm, is a memorial to a young Victorian woman called Fanny Mercer. A servant of a Rugby School master, she fell to her death from the rocks here after tripping over her walking pole.

Croft House
Farm Café

½ mile   1 mile

➡ Walk towards car park entrance and bear **right** when you see Croft House Farm Café diagonally opposite.
➡ When track bends right, ignore route branching right to Scale Force.

1 ➡ Go through gate giving access to Buttermere's shores and turn **right**.
➡ Cross footbridge over lake's outlet stream.

☆ Rock tunnel

George Benson, a 19th-century Manchester industrialist and owner of the Hassness Estate, used to get frustrated at having to detour round the crag that prevented him from walking a full circuit of Buttermere without straying far from the water's edge. So he got his employees to cut this tunnel through the rock.

Hay Stacks The dark, rocky fell looming over the top end of Buttermere is Hay Stacks. It's not particularly high by Lakeland standards but it's part of a spectacular mountain ridge that separates the Buttermere valley from Ennerdale. Its rugged beauty led the famous guidebook writer Alfred Wainwright to name it as his favourite fell. After his death in 1991, Wainwright's ashes were scattered beside Innominate Tarn, one of the pretty mountain pools dotted about its summit.

Hay Stacks

1½ miles   2 miles

2 ➡ Cross second bridge and go through gate into woods.
➡ Bear **left** along lakeshore path for ½ mile, ignoring path climbing straight ahead.

3 ➡ Where narrower path goes left along shore, take middle path, a stony track.
➡ After leaving woods and crossing footbridge, keep **left** when another path heads up to right.

4 ➡ At signposted path junction, turn **left** through gate.
➡ Near buildings of Gatesgarth Farm, walkers are funnelled along fenced path to left of farmyard.

NATURE NOTES

Highland cattle like grazing on the fells

The shores of Buttermere and the surrounding fells are grazed by sheep, mostly the local Herdwick breed, and a small herd of **Highland cattle,** but you'll see wildlife too. Woodland birds include **great spotted woodpecker** and, in the summer, **pied flycatcher**. During the spring, **sandpipers** nest on the shingle beaches of Buttermere and neighbouring Crummock Water. Watch too for the tall, slender Buttermere **pine trees** near the road section of the walk.

Sandpipers are often seen on the shingle beaches around Buttermere

Fanny Mercer

5

2½ miles

6

Rock Tunnel

3 miles

5 ➤ Turn **left** along road.
➤ After about 500 yards, you'll have lake on your left again.

6 ➤ About 120 yards after road bends right, take path signposted **left**.
➤ Keep close to shore for just over 1 mile, later passing through tunnel near Hassness House.

Stands of pines are a familar sight in the Lake District

The great spotted woodpecker's tongue is really long

Some Herdwick sheep stay out on the fells all winter

8
4 miles **Buttermere**
3½ miles **7**
Syke Farm
Tea Room
Fish Inn

7 ➤ At far end of lake, bear **right** when path splits. Route soon climbs steps cut into rock. Follow signs back to village.

8 ➤ At top of fenced section of path, turn **left**.
➤ Go **left** at road.
➤ Turn **left** again just before Bridge Hotel and bear **right** to re-enter car park.

ULLSWATER SHORE

This walk explores a delightful section of the waymarked Ullswater Way beside one of Lakeland's most spectacular bodies of water. Starting from Glenridding at the foot of high, rocky fells, it follows a trail along Ullswater's wooded shoreline to Glencoyne Bay where a well-constructed path leads to the Aira Force car park. From here, catch the 508 bus back to Glenridding or hop on the Ullswater 'Steamers'.

Distance	2.5 miles/4km
Time	1¼ hours (excluding bus or steamer ride)
Start	Glenridding, from car park
Finish	Bus stop near Aira Point (pier for steamer close by)
Parking CA11 0PD	Lake District National Park pay-and-display car park in Glenridding
Public toilets	At start, and just beyond end of route at Aira Force car park
Cafés/pubs	In Glenridding; café at Aira Force car park
Terrain	Wooded shoreline trail and well-constructed path 🏠 Four main road crossings and a 200-yard section of pavementless main road
Hilliness	One climb and descent, after ½ mile
Footwear	All year 👟

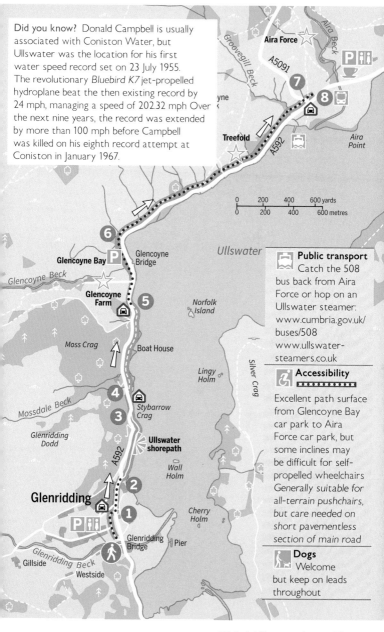

Did you know? Donald Campbell is usually associated with Coniston Water, but Ullswater was the location for his first water speed record set on 23 July 1955. The revolutionary *Bluebird K7* jet-propelled hydroplane beat the then existing record by 24 mph, managing a speed of 202.32 mph Over the next nine years, the record was extended by more than 100 mph before Campbell was killed on his eighth record attempt at Coniston in January 1967.

Aira Force

A5091

Treefold

A592

Aira Point

Ullswater

0 | 200 | 400 | 600 yards
0 | 200 | 400 | 600 metres

Glencoyne Bridge

Glencoyne Bay

Glencoyne Beck

Glencoyne Farm

Norfolk Island

Moss Crag

Boat House

Lingy Holm

Silver Crag

Mossdale Beck

Stybarrow Crag

Glenridding Dodd

Ullswater shorepath

Wall Holm

Glenridding

Cherry Holm

Glenridding Beck

Glenridding Bridge | Pier

Gillside

Westside

Public transport
Catch the 508 bus back from Aira Force or hop on an Ullswater steamer: www.cumbria.gov.uk/buses/508
www.ullswater-steamers.co.uk

Accessibility
Excellent path surface from Glencoyne Bay car park to Aira Force car park, but some inclines may be difficult for self-propelled wheelchairs *Generally suitable for all-terrain pushchairs, but care needed on short pavementless section of main road*

Dogs
Welcome but keep on leads throughout

Walk 4 Ullswater shore **35**

STORIES BEHIND THE WALK

☆ Aira Force waterfall Located just off the main route, it's well worth a visit, particularly after heavy rain when the 65-foot (20-m) white-water drop is at its thunderous best. The trails leading from the car park up to the waterfall are managed by the National Trust, as is the surrounding arboretum with its many unusual trees.

Ullswater Ullswater is the Lake District National Park's second largest body of water, snaking for eight glorious miles from Glenridding to Pooley Bridge. It is fed by streams that come crashing down from the nearby fells, including Helvellyn, England's third highest mountain. One of the best ways to see the lake and the impressive scenery surrounding it is from the Ullswater 'Steamers', which carry passengers between Glenridding, Aira Force, Howtown and Pooley Bridge all year round.

Ullswater shorepath

½ mile

➡ Walk to car park's vehicle entrance and take path to left of 'no exit' sign. This follows loop road to A592.

1 ➡ Cross main road and turn **left** along pavement.

2 ➡ Just after low wall on right ends, turn **right** along trail, descending steps to lakeshore. You now follow waymarked 'Ullswater Way' until path junction after **7**

☆ **Glencoyne Farm** You can see Glencoyne Farm squatting near the base of the fells as you cross the main road at ⑤. Covering more than 3,000 acres, it's one of the National Trust's largest Lake District farms. Parts of the farmhouse date back to 1629, and its round chimneys are typical of old buildings in the area.

☆ **Treefold**

The wood pastures of Glencoyne Park are home to 'Treefold: North', an art installation created by Harriet and Rob Fraser in 2017. They used dry-stone walling techniques to build a circular fold containing a single oak. The stones are carved with words that combine with two other 'treefolds' in Cumbria to make up a poem.

Glencoyne Farm ☆

④ · · · · · · · · · · · · · ·

1 mile

③ ➡When path leads back up to road, continue in same direction on asphalt for 200 yards.

④ ➡At far end of small lay-by to right of road, step on to path on **right**. Stay on main path, running parallel with A592 for another ⅓ mile.

NATURE NOTES

You're never far from trees on this walk – along Ullswater's wooded shoreline and in Glencoyne's wood pastures. **Red squirrels** thrive here, attracted in part by the variety of species. As well as large trees, including **oak**, there is a rich understorey containing species such as **holly**. Resident waterfowl include **mute swans** and **moorhens**. The area's **daffodils**, common in spring, are said to have inspired William Wordsworth's famous poem, although not all are of the native 'Lent lily' variety.

Unusally, barnacle geese have been known to stay on the lake during the summer months

Whooper swans also come to Ullswater to mix with the mute swans. They have bright yellow beaks

P   1½ miles

5 ➥ When roadside route ends, cross over and turn **right** along enclosed path.
➥ Cross farm lane to continue on path to reach Glencoyne Bay car park.

6 ➥ At far end of car park, cross two footbridges in quick succession to join path through Glencoyne Park.
➥ Carry on for just over 1 mile to A5091.

William Wordsworth's inspiration, daffodils are a common sight in early spring

11,000 trees have been planted around Ullswater to combat climate change; species include holly

Violets flower from March to May – look out for them in woods and hedgerows

☆ Treefold

2 miles

7 ➥ Cross main road and take path opposite. In just 50 yards, turn **right** at signposted path junction.

8 ➥ Bus stop back to Glenridding is on far side of road (A592). For Ullswater 'Steamers', use gate beside bus stop and follow path to pier.

This page (clockwise): meadow brown (left) and ringlet butterflies; mute swan on Derwent Water; red squirrel; Herdwick sheep in bracken Opposite: Rydal Water at dawn; bluebells overlooking Ullswater; red deer; great spotted woodpecker

GRASMERE

It's no wonder that England's favourite Romantic poet, William Wordsworth, chose to live most of his life within a pebble's throw of Grasmere, one of the National Park's smallest and prettiest lakes. Visiting one of his homes and his final resting place en route, this walk starts in Grasmere village and uses quiet lanes, trails through mature oak woodland and a tranquil waterside path to complete a full circuit of the lake.

Distance	3.8 miles/6.1km
Time	2 hours
Start/Finish	Stock Lane car park, off B5287, Grasmere village
Parking LA22 9SJ	Lake District pay-and-display car park at Stock Lane, Grasmere
Public toilets	At start; close by ③ White Moss car park
Cafés/pubs	In Grasmere
Terrain	Lanes, woodland trails and lakeshore path. 🏠 Two main road crossings
Hilliness	Undulating on lanes; one rise from shore path after 2¾ miles
Footwear	All year 🥾

Did you know? Artistic tourism gained popularity in the 18th century. Famous visitors to Grasmere included John Constable and JMW Turner.

Local legend Sadly, Grasmere's annual Guzzler Festival had to be cancelled in 2020. Started in 2006, it is held over three days on the first weekend in September. There is plenty of music and some 120 beers available, all accompanied by food stalls cooking local produce. An even older event is the Grasmere Gallop: held annually for the last 35 years, it offers a variety of running trails from 3½ to 26¼ miles and even a Teddy Dash for under-fives.

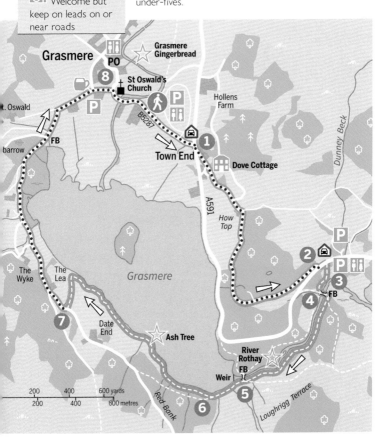

STORIES BEHIND
THE WALK

🏠 **Dove Cottage** This white-washed cottage, which started life as an inn known as the Dove and Olive, was the home of William Wordsworth and his growing family from 1799 until 1808. This is where the poet wrote some of his best-known verse, including *I Wandered Lonely as a Cloud* (or 'Daffodils'). When he moved out, his tenancy was taken up by his young friend Thomas de Quincey, famous for his autobiographical work *Confessions of an English Opium-Eater*.

☆ **River Rothay** This section of the River Rothay, popular with kayakers and canoeists, links the two lakes, Grasmere and Rydal Water. Barely 10 miles long, the Rothay begins life on the fells north of Grasmere and drains into Windermere.

Dove Cottage

➡ Turn **left** out of car park – along Stock Lane.
➡ At mini-roundabout on A591, turn **right**.

1 ➡ Immediately take lane on **left**.
➡ At signposted T-junction in 450 yards, stay on lane in 'White Moss and Ambleside' direction for just over ½ mile, with lake views to right.

2 ➡ Reaching main road, go **left** for 50 yards. (Safer to pass through car park, parallel to A591.)
➡ Then pass through low wall gap diagonally left from car park entrance.

☆ Wordsworth graves

There are several sites in Grasmere and nearby Rydal that are closely linked with Wordsworth, including St Oswald's Church. This is where the poet, who died in 1850 aged 80, and several members of his family are buried. Their simple graves are located towards the back of the churchyard.

☆ Grasmere Gingerbread

Grasmere's famous gingerbread has been made on the same site and to the same recipe since 1854. This is when Sarah Nelson moved into the old village school beside St Oswald's Church and began selling her spicy concoction to the tourists visiting the Lake District in growing numbers. Just as popular today, the gingerbread recipe remains a closely guarded secret.

☆ River Rothay

3 ➤ After descending stony steps, turn **right** at T-junction of paths near River Rothay.

4 ➤ Cross bridge and immediately turn **right** along riverside path through woods.

NATURE NOTES

Grasmere is beautiful all year round, but it's at it best in the autumn when the trees, including **oak**, begin to shed their leaves. Spring is gorgeous too, when the slope leading up from the beach is carpeted in **bluebells** and the yellow of **lesser celandine**, the subject of a Wordsworth poem, bring colour to the woodland floor. **Roe deer** frequent the woods and **herons** the river and lake. Watch for an interesting old **ash tree** with hollowed-out trunk beside the shore path.

This old ash tree could be mistaken for one of Tolkien's ents from *The Lord of the Rings*

There is a heronry on the island in the middle of the lake, but they can often be seen fishing on the River Rothay

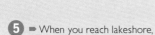

Ash
☆ tree

6

2 miles

7

5 ➡ When you reach lakeshore, cross shingle beach.
➡ At woodland edge, follow stony path rising from shore.

6 ➡ When route ahead splits, keep **right**, along lakeside path.
➡ In just over ½ mile, the path turns sharp left and climbs to lane.

Early morning or late evening are the best times of day to spot a roe deer

Wordsworth named one of his poems after the little celandine, which flowers from February until May

Glorious autumn colours reflected in Grasmere

Grasmere Gingerbread ☆   St Oswald's Church

8

3 miles

7 ➡ Turn **right** along road and stroll for 1 mile to Grasmere village.

8 ➡ Turn **right** at T-junction opposite churchyard. Car park entrance is on left in 300 yards.

ESKDALE

Hidden away in the western Lakes, Eskdale is one of the National Park's quietest valleys – and yet it has much to offer visitors willing to make the effort required to reach it. This walk uses the area's recently improved path network to explore its tranquil middle reaches. As well as wandering the wooded banks of the River Esk and following the route of an old tramway, it visits an ancient church and a restored watermill.

Distance	2 miles/3.2km
Time	1 hour
Start/Finish	Dalegarth for Boot Station
Parking CA19 1TF	Pay-and-display car park at Dalegarth for Boot Station
Public toilets	For patrons at station only
Cafés/pubs	Café at Dalegarth for Boot Station; pubs in Boot village
Terrain	Lanes and good tracks
Hilliness	Very gently undulating
Footwear	All year ➣

Did you know? The Boot Inn, Eskdale, was originally called the Burnmoor Inn. A quick search reveals that this was a popular destination with walking groups in the 1970s due to the eccentricities of the landlady, Big Josie. Josie Heap was Austrian and a superb cook. Meals were accompanied by very colourful language and not many clothes!

Local legend Roughly a quarter of a mile from St Catherine's Church in Boot lies Arment Hill; in the sixth century a hermit lived there and the water from his well is still used for baptisms in the church.

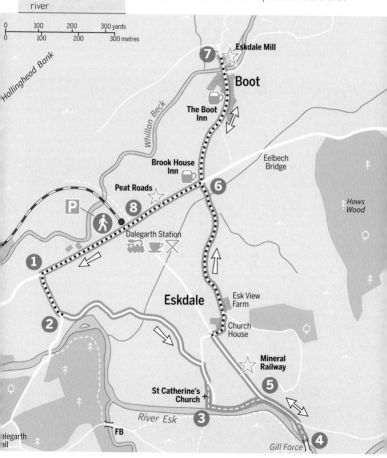

STORIES BEHIND
THE WALK

☆ **Mineral railway** Beyond the gates at ⑤ you follow the route of an old tramway. This was built in the 1880s to carry iron ore from mines near the River Esk to the narrow-gauge mineral railway that ran from Dalegarth to Ravenglass. Although the tramway no longer exists, the main part of the valley line is now home to the Ravenglass and Eskdale Railway, known affectionately as the La'al Ratty.

☆ **Peat roads** As you walk the road back to the car park, you might be able to make out a grassy path zig-zagging up the hillside beyond the station. This is one of several old peat roads in Eskdale. Local families would once have dug peat for fuel from the bogs above, dried it out in huts on the moorland edge and then brought it down these gently inclined paths on sledges.

½

➤ Take pedestrian path from end of car park furthest from station building.
➤ Climb steps and turn **right** along road. (Wheelchairs use vehicle access.)

① ➤ Take next lane on **left**, passing war memorial on right. ➤ Walk 125 yards to bend in lane.

✝ St Catherine's Church

Before St Olaf's Church in Wasdale was licensed for burials, coffins had to be carried across the moody moorland to the medieval St Catherine's Church in Eskdale for interment. The 'corpse road' linking the two valleys can still be followed today, although would-be walkers should be aware it's associated with several ghost stories.

☆ **Eskdale Mill** Eskdale is home to the Lake District's last working water-powered corn mill. The waterwheels and buildings, some of which date back to the 18th century, have been restored and are now open to the public.

St Catherine's ✝ Church

Mineral ☆ railway

1 mile

2 ▸ On meeting path and fingerpost, drop **left** – through gate – along path to St Catherine's Church.
▸ Turn **right** at T-junction with broad track to reach church.

3 ▸ Just after church, bear **left** beside River Esk.
▸ Turn **right** after gate.
▸ At next fingerpost, follow riverside path to footbridge.

NATURE NOTES

Eskdale's woodland is one of the last English bastions of the native **red squirrel**, largely displaced in the rest of the country by the North American grey. **Peregrine falcons** nest in the valley, and, if you're out at twilight, you might be lucky enough to spot **badgers**. In spring, watch for dainty yellow **primroses** beside the paths. In autumn, flocks of **fieldfare** flit from one **hawthorn** tree to another, stripping them of their red, berry-like fruit.

Fieldfare migrate from Scandinavia, arriving in October and leaving in March. They are known as the winter thrush

Badger cubs are very curious

The Boot Inn

Brook House Inn

1½ m

1 mile

4 ➡ After enjoying the gorge and river here, turn back and retrace steps for 175 yards.

5 ➡ When you see two sets of gates ahead, go through one on **right**.
➡ Beyond next gate, turn **right** along lane for almost ½ mile to Brook House Inn.

6 ➡ Go **straight over** at crossroads (passing inn on left).
➡ Walk ⅓ mile into village to humpback bridge.

May sees hawthorn burst into blossom. Flowers have five petals and are highly scented

Rowan trees have long been associated with Eskdale. Often wind-swept, they can live for 200 years. Birds are attracted to the bright red berries

Peregrine falcons are super speedy, but you may hear their *kak, kak, kak* call before seeing them

The Boot Inn

dale
ill

Brook
House Inn

Peat
roads
☆

2 miles

7 ➧ Cross bridge to reach Eskdale Mill. After visit, retrace steps to crossroads (Brook House Inn now on right).
➧ Turn **right** and walk 270 yards to Dalegarth Station.

8 ➧ Turn **right** to re-enter station car park where walk started.

WRAY CASTLE & BLELHAM TARN

Setting off from the imposing Wray Castle, walkers are in for a treat on this tranquil route close to the western shores of Windermere. Using a gravel, off-road cycle path for much of the walk's first half, it passes in and out of woodland and flirts with the edge of Blelham Tarn, a little-known body of water where wildlife thrives. The second half follows a series of quiet lanes through the gently rolling landscape, enjoying superb views of Windermere and the surrounding fells.

Distance	4.7 miles/7.6 km
Time	2¾ hours
Start/Finish	Wray Castle, Low Wray
Parking	LA22 0JA National Trust pay-and-display car park at Wray Castle
Public toilets	None. (Toilets at NT café)
Cafés/pubs	Café at Wray Castle
Terrain	Lanes, and paths mostly with improved surfaces
Hilliness	One steeper rise approaching ❹ and, thereafter, a steady rise to Outgate
Footwear	All year

Did you know? Wray Castle was leased from 1958 to 1998 to the Merchant Navy. The college trained ship's radio operators. This followed the loss of the *Titanic*, after which all ships were required to have trained operators on 24-hour call.

Local legend Canon Hardwicke Rawnsley became vicar at Wray Church in 1878 and went on to become a close friend of Beatrix Potter. He was particularly opposed to the building of a railway to service the Braithwaite slate quarry – a battle he won. He became a local hero and was dubbed 'Defender of the Lakes'. He became one of the founders of the National Trust.

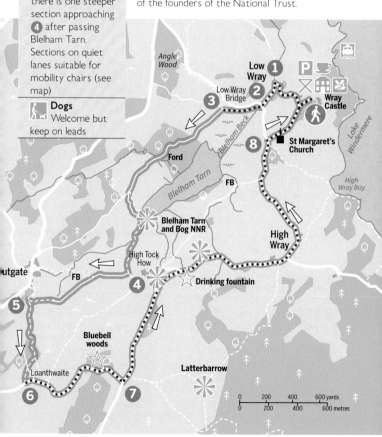

STORIES BEHIND
THE WALK

Wray Castle The mock-Gothic mansion of Wray Castle was built in the 1840s by James Dawson, a retired Liverpool surgeon. He spent much of his wife's inheritance on it, but it's said she took one look at it and refused to live there. Wray Castle was also the location for Beatrix Potter's family's first Lakeland holiday – the place where she first fell in love with the landscape that inspired much of her work. The building, now open to the public, is owned by the National Trust.

Blelham Tarn and Bog NNR The bog surrounding Blelham Tarn is a National Nature Reserve, protected because of the important species that live here. These include a number of rare invertebrates, several sphagnum mosses and bog myrtle, the aromatic leaves of which can be used to ward off midges.

Wray Castle

➤ Walk back along castle's access drive. Soon after passing Dower House B&B, take path on **right** descending to hamlet of Low Wray.

1 ➤ Nearing buildings, follow gravel path round to left and then turn **left** along surfaced lane.
➤ Stroll to lane junction.

☆ Drinking fountain

Just after passing the second lane down to High Tock How, you will see an ornate water fountain, made largely from slate, to the right of the road. Dated 1891 and bearing the inscription, 'In memory of happy days', the fountain is a Grade II Listed Building.

※ Windermere There
are several points from where Windermere can be seen, the best viewpoints being on the road section of the walk. England's largest natural lake, it is almost 11 miles long. The fells that can be seen on the far side of the water include those making up the Fairfield Horseshoe, one of the Lake District's most popular mountain walks.

elham Tarn
d Bog NNR

2 miles

2 ➡ Turn **right** and immediately go through gate on **left** to join off-road section of National Cycle Network's Route 6 to gate in 200 yards.

3 ➡ Go **left** through gate (following Route 6's Hawkshead spur to **6**).
➡ Keep to surfaced path for 1 mile, through several gates, ignoring two right turnings, to reach gate by barn.

NATURE NOTES

In terms of wildlife, Blelham Tarn is the highlight of this walk. **Great crested grebes** breed on the tarn and, in the autumn, **whooper swans** fly in from the Arctic to spend the winter here. Come spring, much of the woodland is bedecked with **bluebells**, and you might also see **violets** growing beside the path. In summer, watch for the fluffy white heads of **bog cotton**, or cotton grass, swaying in the breeze and the flowers of another bog plant, **white beak sedge**.

The spectacular courtship of great crested grebes

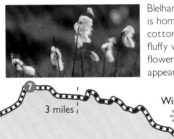

Blelham Tarn is home to bog cotton. The fluffy white flower heads appear in June

Bluebell woods ☆

7

3 miles

Windermere views ✳ ✳

☆

Drinking fountai

4 ➡ At barn, go through gate, continue to top of rise and then turn **right** at path junction.
➡ Stay on clear path for nearly ½ mile to Outgate.

5 ➡ At T-junction of paths, just below cottages at Outgate, turn **left** through gate.
➡ Follow path to Loanthwaite, halfway along passing through deciduous woodland.

6 ➡ Walk **left** and stride out to next lane T-junction.

Spectacular bluebell woods abound in the Lake District, Wray Castle is no exception

White beak sedge

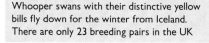

Whooper swans with their distinctive yellow bills fly down for the winter from Iceland. There are only 23 breeding pairs in the UK

High Wray

4 miles

St Margaret's Church

Wray Castle

7 ▪ Slip **left** again.
▪ Continue on lane for 1½ miles to gates of Wray Castle, ignoring two lanes on left to High Tock How and turning on right to Windermere Ferry, and pass through High Wray.

8 ▪ Turn **right** through gateway and follow access drive back to car park.

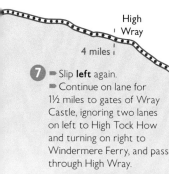

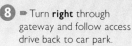

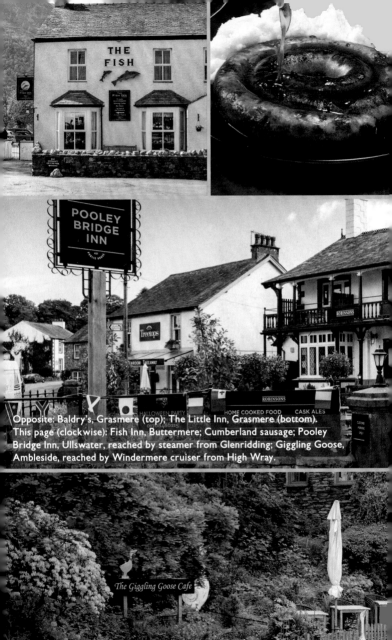

Opposite: Baldry's, Grasmere (top); The Little Inn, Grasmere (bottom).
This page (clockwise): Fish Inn, Buttermere; Cumberland sausage; Pooley
Bridge Inn, Ullswater, reached by steamer from Glenridding; Giggling Goose,
Ambleside, reached by Windermere cruiser from High Wray.

GRIZEDALE FOREST

Who can resist a walk in the woods? And, at the Lake District's largest forestry site, you'll really feel like the trees go on forever. This walk keeps to waymarked tracks and trails as it explores Grizedale Forest. Views of the surrounding fells come and go as you pass through open areas, and there's plenty of opportunity for wildlife spotting. The visitor centre, where the walk begins and ends, has facilities that include a café and children's adventure play area.

Distance	5 miles/8.1km
Time	2¾ hours
Start/Finish	Grizedale
Parking	LA22 0QJ Grizedale Forest Visitor Centre pay-and-display car park
Public toilets	At visitor centre
Cafés/pubs	Visitor centre café
Terrain	Good forest tracks and paths
Hilliness	Steady ascent over first mile, then gently undulating for 2 miles, and gently descending for 2 miles
Footwear	All year 👞

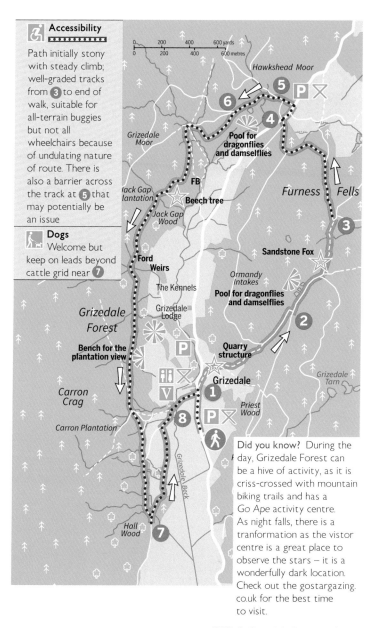

Dogs
Welcome but keep on leads beyond cattle grid near **7**

0   200   400   600 yards
0   200   400   600 metres

Hawkshead Moor

5 P ✕

6

4

Pool for dragonflies and damselflies

Grizedale Moor

Furness Fells

Jack Gap Plantation

FB

Jack Gap Wood

Beech tree

3

Ford

Weirs

Sandstone Fox

The Kennels

Ormandy Intakes

Pool for dragonflies and damselflies

Grizedale Forest

Grizedale Lodge

2

Bench for the plantation view

P

Quarry structure

Grizedale Tarn

♿ ✕
V

Grizedale

1

P ✕

Carron Crag

🚶

Priest Wood

Carron Plantation

8

Grizedale Beck

Did you know? During the day, Grizedale Forest can be a hive of activity, as it is criss-crossed with mountain biking trails and has a Go Ape activity centre. As night falls, there is a tranformation as the vistor centre is a great place to observe the stars – it is a wonderfully dark location. Check out the gostargazing. co.uk for the best time to visit.

Hall Wood

7

STORIES BEHIND THE WALK

☆ Sculptures

There are dozens of sculptures and art installations scattered throughout the sprawling Grizedale Forest. You'll pass several on this walk, including 'Quarry Structure' to the right of the path soon after you set off. This is one of the oldest works, created by Richard Harris in 1977. Watch too for 'Red Sandstone Fox', sculpted by Gordon Young in 1991.

🌿 Coppicing

Before the plantations, much of the Grizedale woodland would have been coppiced – a management technique used to stimulate growth and provide a sustainable supply of timber. Coppicers cut the timber by hand. It was used locally for charcoal burning, bobbin making and iron smelting.

Pool for dragonflies and damselflies 🌿

1 mile

☆ Red sandstone fox

Quarry structure ☆

P V
🍴 🏛
🍴

➡ Head to top end of car park (to visitor centre) and turn **right** along road.

1 ➡ In a few strides, immediately after building on right, take gravel track rising to **right** of road.
➡ In ⅓ mile keep **straight ahead** on joining forest track from left.
➡ Reach T-junction in 375 yards.

2 ➡ Turn **left**. At next junction, with fox sculpture on left, go **straight over**.
➡ Almost immediately, take narrower path signposted **left** and follow it for 500 yards to broad track junction on sweeping bend.

☆ Mountain biking

Mountain bikers of all abilities find plenty to entertain and challenge them at Grizedale. While the well-graded forest roads and tracks are great for novices and families in search of some off-road cycling fun, the more experienced will opt for the red- or black-graded single-track trails with their jumps, berms and rapid descents.

☆ Plantations

Grizedale is the Lake District's largest Forestry England site. The area has been woodland for centuries, but the conifer plantations date back only to the 1930s. They now consist largely of Sitka spruce, many of the larch trees having been felled because they had ramorum disease. The walk passes through several plantations, and there is a particularly good view of the conifers on the eastern side of the forest from the carved memorial bench, created by artist Nigel Ross, between **6** and **7**.

2 miles | Pool for dragonflies and damselflies

3 ➤ Turn **left** and remain on broad track for ½ mile to next main junction.
➤ Turn **right**, dropping downhill to road.

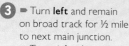

4 ➤ At road, turn **right**. In 140 yards, go **left** along Moor Top car park's access drive.

NATURE NOTES

You may get lucky and spot a fox cub

You'll need to open your senses to a huge range of potential encounters in the forest. Of course, there are trees —the gnarly old **beech** to the left of the track between ⑥ and ⑦ is a fabulous example — and **treecreepers** can often be seen spiralling up their trunks. **Foxes** can be spotted and, in late summer and autumn, **fly agaric** is one of the most common fungi on the forest floor. Watch the skies for **red kites**, released here in 2010. There are also several shallow pools where colourful **dragonflies and damselflies** can be spotted.

A male banded demoiselle

☆ Beech tree

3 miles

Bench for plantation vie

⑥ ➤ Reaching fork, bear **left**, heading downhill. Follow broad forest track for further 2¼ miles, ignoring several paths/tracks off to left and right, ultimately coming to T-junction near woodland edge.

⑤ ➤ Immediately after barrier, bear **left** as track splits.
➤ Shortly, as another path joins from right, bend **left** with the ongoing track and continue to next fork.

What stories this ancient beech tree could tell!

Red kite

Fly agaric

Golden-ringed dragonfly

4 miles

5 miles

7 ➡ Go **left** – soon going through gate beside cattle grid.
➡ Keep on for almost ½ mile to next set of gates.

8 ➡ Through gates, **turn** right along farm lane.
➡ At road, cross **diagonally left**, walking between bollards to return to car park.

V P
⌗ ✕

CONISTON

The slender ribbon of Coniston Water stretches for five miles through the rolling countryside of the South Lakes. Setting off from the north-west shore, walkers enjoy the views down the lake before heading into Coniston village. Beyond the historic church of St Andrew's and the Ruskin Museum, the route makes for the base of rugged fells before returning, along a rough beckside path, to the lake – where a waterside café awaits those who have worked up a thirst.

Distance	2.9 miles/4.6km
Time	1½ hours
Start/Finish	Coniston Boating Centre
Parking LA21 8AN	Coniston Boating Centre pay-and-display car park, Lake Road, Coniston
Public toilets	At start
Cafés/pubs	Café at lakeshore; cafés and pubs in Coniston village
Terrain	Field paths, village pavements and stony tracks
Hilliness	Steady climb to Miners Bridge, ❹, and descent back into village
Footwear	All year 👞

Did you know? In the 12th century, Coniston was know as Coningeston. It is believed that this comes from the old norse word for king – *konungr*.

Local legend Lots of places in the Lake District have associations with giants, and Coniston is no exception. Girt Will o the Tarns was roughly nine feet tall. He made the mistake of falling in love with Barbara, the Laird of Coniston Hall's daughter. Already engaged to Dick Hawksley, she rejected Will, and while walking with her mother, Will abducted her. Dick and the Laird set off in hot pursuit and caught the pair at Kernel Dub, just to the north of Coniston. The girl fell in the Yewdale Beck and was swept away with Dick, only to emerge from the lake a week later. Will was killed by the Laird's men. Legend has it that the mound beside the beck is his grave.

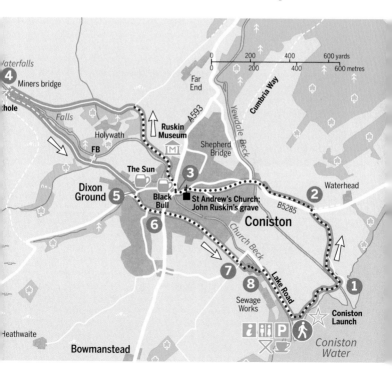

STORIES BEHIND THE WALK

☆ **Water speed records** Several world water speed records were broken on Coniston Water in the 20th century. Malcolm Campbell achieved 141mph in August 1939, and then his son Donald set one record after another during the 1950s and 1960s. In January 1967, while attempting to break the 300mph barrier, Donald's jet boat Bluebird K7 did a backward somersault and then nose-dived into the lake, killing him instantly.

John Ruskin

One of the most influential thinkers of the 19th century, his ideas led to the formation of the National Trust and influenced the early development of the Labour Party. He lived at Brantwood on the shores of Coniston Water and is buried in St Andrew's churchyard. His grave is marked by a large cross made from local slate.

½ mile

➡ Walk towards lake from car park and turn **left** along gravel path beside kiosk.

1 ➡ Cross bridge.
➡ Where path joins driveway, bear **left**.

☆ Coniston Launch

The boats of the Coniston Launch ply their way up and down the lake, laden with sightseers, all year round. In summer, a themed 'Swallows and Amazons' cruise visits Peel Island, which became Wild Cat Island in Arthur Ransome's book – the place to where the fictional Walker children sailed their dinghy 'Swallow' and set up camp.

🏛 Ruskin Museum

Coniston's Ruskin Museum includes exhibits on Donald Campbell, John Ruskin and Arthur Ransome, whose *Swallows and Amazons* children's adventure stories were set in the area. It also tells the story of the miners and quarrymen who started extracting minerals from the surrounding mountains on an industrial scale from Elizabethan times onwards.

St Andrew's Church and John Ruskin's grave † ■

Black Bull 🍵

Ruskin Museum 🏛

1 mile

2 ➡ At road, cross over and turn **left** along shared-use path.
➡ When this ends, continue 350 yards to village centre on road and then pavement.

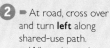

3 ➡ At T-junction with A593, turn **right** and then go **left** immediately after Black Bull.
➡ Stay on this lane, surfaced at first, becoming rougher as it climbs, for over ½ mile to gated bridge.

NATURE NOTES

This walk gives a taste of the wildlife associated with both lake and fells. Watch for various birds on and around Coniston Water, including **mallards** and **black-headed gulls**. On summer evenings, **swifts** fly low and fast over the lake, catching insects. As you head towards the fells, you'll see a fern called **bracken** on the lower slopes. A rich green in summer, it turns a coppery colour in autumn. Watch too for **holly** beside the paths. Immediately after crossing Miners Bridge, there's a distinctive **knothole** in a tree trunk on your right.

Birds known as cavity nesters take up home in trees with knotholes

4 ☆ Knothole tree

1½ miles

2 miles

4 ➡ Known as Miners Bridge, use it to cross Church Beck.
➡ Immediately turn **left**, descending back to Coniston on broad, stony path.

5 ➡ Beyond farmyard at Dixon Ground, join lane.
➡ With The Sun pub on left, turn **right** along road and go **left** at next junction.

6 ➡ At crossroads with main road, go **straight over** – along Lake Road – and proceed to sharp left bend in about 450 yards.

The black-headed gull's head is actually only black in summer— it turns white in winter

The arrival of swifts is an early indicator of spring. In 2019 and 2020, they were early, but in 2021 they were much later. Departure dates are much less predictable and depend on insect numbers to feed their chicks

Bracken is poisonous to grazing livestock and small mammals

The Sun

2½ miles

Coniston Launch ☆

7 ➥ At bend, enter Lake Road Estate on **right**.
➥ Turn **left** through gap between two buildings and quickly bear **right** to pick up signed footpath.

8 ➥ Follow footpath to bridge, cross it and turn **right** along road.
➥ Car park is on left in 200 yards.

WALK 10

RAVENGLASS

Did you know the Lake District has a coastline? Not only that, but it also has a pretty little seaside village, called Ravenglass. The Romans knew about it and built a port here. Take a stroll along the England Coast Path to see the remains of the Roman bathhouse and to enjoy the serenity of the village and the estuary. Beware, the 150-yard section of the route beside the River Esk floods at exceptionally high tides.

Distance	2.2 miles/3.5km
Time	1¼ hours
Start/Finish	Ravenglass car park
Parking CA18 1SQ	Lake District National Park pay-and-display car park on Croftlands Drive, Ravenglass (not railway car park)
Public toilets	At start
Cafés/pubs	In Ravenglass; café at Ravenglass and Eskdale Steam Railway
Terrain	Village lane, shore path, beach and good track under trees
Hilliness	Level walking
Footwear	All year 👢

Did you know? Until 2007, the local railway known as La'al Ratty held an annual *Day out with Thomas* with the 'Wroxham Broad' playing *Thomas the Tank Engine*. It is hoped that more of these will be held in the future.

Local legend Muncaster Castle has overlooked Ravenglass since Roman times. It is said to be home to ghost Tom Skelton, otherwise known as Tom Fool, who was a jester in the castle towards the end of the 16th century. Legend has it that he had a penchant for playing nasty tricks on people, and was even responsible for the murder of a local carpenter.

Public transport
Train connections from Carlisle and Lancaster: see www.nationalrail.co.uk

Accessibility
Good on road through village and along Walls Drive to/from Roman bathhouse; suitable for all-terrain pushchairs, except on viaduct

Dogs
Welcome but keep on leads beside roads and estuary

STORIES BEHIND THE WALK

☘ Drigg dunes
The Drigg dunes nature reserve, visible on the other side of the estuary from the path to Saltcoats, is notable for its variety of habitats. These include the dunes themselves, salt marsh, wetland and mudflats. These are home to a range of amphibians (including great crested newts and natterjack toads), unusual invertebrates, salt-tolerant plants and various bird species.

☘ Irish Sea coast
Ravenglass is the only coastal village within the Lake District National Park. It sits on an estuary where three rivers meet – the Esk, Mitre and Irt. On a clear day, from higher points on this section of the coast, it's possible to look out across the Irish Sea to the Isle of Man.

Dring dunes

½ m

1 ➡ From car park, follow Croftlands Drive back down to waterfront and bend **right**.
➡ With estuary on left, walk to railway bridge.

1 ➡ Just before bridge, turn **left** along footpath signposted 'Saltcoats'. Part of the England Coast Path, this crosses viaduct and soon bends left paralleling the shoreline.

La'al Ratty

Ravenglass is the western terminus of the La'al Ratty heritage line, more formally known as the Ravenglass and Eskdale Railway. (La'al is local dialect for 'little'.) The narrow-gauge railway was built in 1875 to carry iron ore from Eskdale's mines to the main line on the coast. Today, steam engines take passengers on the seven-mile journey from Ravenglass, up into beautiful Eskdale, as far as Dalegarth (Boot).

Roman bathhouse

Ravenglass was home to a Roman fort and port, called Glannaventa. Troops and supplies would have been brought in to maintain garrisons throughout north-west England, while lead, mined in the Lake District may well have been shipped out to other parts of the empire. All that remains of the Roman settlement today are some earthworks and the substantial bathhouse ruins, now known as Walls Castle.

The Inn at Ravenglass

3 ————————————————— 4

1 mile

2 ➡ When the path widens at fingerpost, turn **right**.
➡ Walk along edge of salt marsh as far as road-end near caravan park, taking in estuary views.

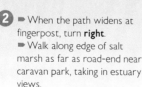

3 ➡ Turn around and retrace steps. Beyond viaduct, turn **right** at road, still following 'England Coast Path' signs to reach Croftlands Drive.

NATURE NOTES

Little egrets, often seen on the estuary, have been breeding in the UK since the 1980s, gradually extending their range northwards. Other birds that frequent the mudflats and salt marshes include **oystercatchers** and **ringed plovers**. In spring, listen for the loud and prolonged song of the **skylark**, performed by males as they rise almost vertically into the air. **Thrift**, or sea pink, grows on the salt marshes, attracting a range of butterflies, including the **common blue**.

Little egret are seen in winter on the mud flats

When ringed plover sense danger to their chicks, they feign a broken wing to lead the predator away from the nest

Irish Sea coast

Beach

Roman bathhouse

1½ mile

4 ➤ As Croftlands Drive bends left (back to car park), keep **ahead** on Main Street to its end.
➤ Descend slipway and then turn **left** along beach for 150 yards. (Flooded at exceptionally high tides.)

5 ➤ Where England Coast Path goes right, keep **straight on**, passing to left of water treatment works. Watch your head as you pass under low railway bridge!

Oystercatchers' main source of food is molluscs such as mussels. A quick jab with their beaks opens the shells with ease

8

2 miles

6 ➤ At surfaced lane, go **right**, immediately **left** and **right** again along trail through trees – here joining alternative route of England Coast Path to reach Roman site, Walls Castle.

7 ➤ After viewing ruins, turn round and retrace steps to ➤ This time, keep **ahead** following trail until it ends, then continue in same direction along lane almost to its end.

8 ➤ Immediately after two stone gateposts either side of lane, go **left** along enclosed path. After pedestrian bridge over railway, bear **right** to re-enter car park.

Publishing information

OS GetOutside Champion:
Craig Henderson

OS content: Helen Newman, Liz Beverley

© Crown copyright 2021.
All rights reserved.

Ordnance Survey, OS, the OS logos and GetOutside are registered trademarks, and OS Short Walks Made Easy is a trademark of Ordnance Survey Ltd.

© Crown copyright and database rights (2021) Ordnance Survey.

ISBN 978 0 319092 24 8
1st edition published by Ordnance Survey 2021.

www.ordnancesurvey.co.uk

While every care has been taken to ensure the accuracy of the route directions, the publishers cannot accept responsibility for errors or omissions, or for changes in details given. The countryside is not static: hedges and fences can be removed, stiles can be replaced by gates, field boundaries can alter, footpaths can be rerouted and changes in ownership can result in the closure or diversion of some concessionary paths. Also, paths that are easy and pleasant for walking in fine conditions may become slippery, muddy and difficult in wet weather.

If you find an inaccuracy in either the text or maps, please contact Ordnance Survey at os.uk/contact.

A catalogue record for this book is available from the British Library.

Trotman Publishing credits

Series editor: Kevin Freeborn

Author: Vivienne Crow

Maps: Cosmographics

Design and Production: Patrick Dawson, Trotman Publishing

Printed in the UK by Ashford Colour Press

Photography credits

Front cover ©Garry Basnett/stock.adobe.com. **Back cover** Monkey Business Images/Shutterstock.com.

All photographs supplied by the author © Vivienne Crow except page 6 Ordnance Survey; 9, 28 ©Harry Johnson Photography/LDNPA; 17, 31 Kris McKenzie; 28 © Andrew Locking/LDNPA; 28, 29 ©John Hodgson/LDNPA; 29 ©Lake District National Park Authority; 39 Patrick Dawson.

The following images were supplied by Shutterstock.com: page 1 Jo McGrath; 5 Geof Leigh; 7 Mark Burn; 15 Iordanis; 16 Anne Elizabeth Mitchell; 18 Hanahstocks; 18 Nick Vorobey; 18 Samvel Hovsepyan; 19 Glenn R Gregory; 19 Ihor Hvozdetskyi; 19 sunakri; 24 godi photo; 24 jack perks; 25 Benjamin B; 25 Cristian Mihai; 25 Daniele Caneve; 32 Neil Bowman; 33 Luka Hercigonja; 36 David Steele; 36 MNStudio; 38 Maxim Nikiforov; 40 andrewcarter901; 40 Glenn R Gregory; 40 MarkLG; 40 Rick Ollerton; 41 Christopher Czermak; 41 Eleanor Hamilton; 41 Matt Gibson; 41 PhilMacDPhoto; 45 Joyce Nelson; 47 365_visuals; 47 Kaprisova; 52 Coatesy; 52 Dark_Side; 53 Chris Hill; 53 ian driscoll; 53 O de R; 57 Ruslan Zaitsau; 58 Tom Pilgrim; 58 Wang LiQiang; 59 Mickmorg; 59 mizy; 59 Ondrej Prosicky; 60 Dani Berszt; 60 JohnGK; 60 SteAck; 60 tipwam; 61 Joyce Nelson; 64 David Ridley; 65 Scott Clarence; 66 Graham Taylor; 66 Sarah L Woods; 67 BartTa; 67 Keith Hider; 67 Paolo-manzi; 70 Steven Webling; 73 Hami Shri; 73 Sokolov Alexey; 74 Geof Leigh; 78 tahirsphotography; 78 Zhang Hanwen; 79 rock ptarmigan.